Birtley Library
16 Durham Road
Birtley
County Durham
DH3 1LE
0191 433 6101

Due for Return	Due for Return	Due for Return
15 MAR 2011		
-1 FEB	1 4 MAR 2024	
1 2 AUG 2014 27 JUL 2022		
1 4 OCT 2023	1 6 MAY 2016	

Visit us at:

www.gateshead.gov.uk/books

Tel: 0191 433 8400

C1 693990 60

The most famous job in history?

Mummy Maker

the BIG PICTURE

Anna Claybourne

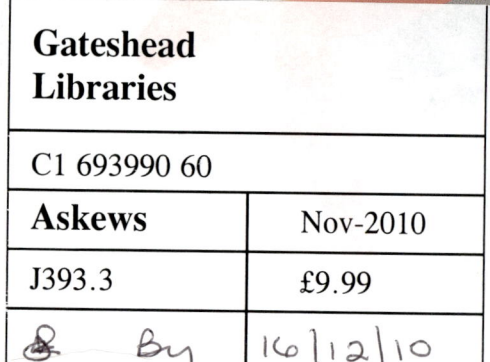

Published 2010 by
A&C Black Publishers Ltd.
36 Soho Square, London, W1D 3QY

www.acblack.com

ISBN HB 978-1-4081-2793-3
       PB 978-1-4081-3156-5

Text copyright © 2010 Anna Claybourne

The right of Anna Claybourne to be identified as the author of this work has been asserted by her in accordance with the Copyrights, Designs and Patents Act 1988.

A CIP catalogue for this book is available from the British Library.

All rights reserved. No part of this publication may be reproduced in any form or by any means – graphic, electronic or mechanical, including photocopying, recording, taping or information storage and retrieval systems – without the prior permission in writing of the publishers.

Every effort has been made to trace copyright holders and to obtain their permission for use of copyright material. The author and publishers would be pleased to rectify any error or omission in future editions.

This book is produced using paper that is made from wood grown in managed, sustainable forests. It is natural, renewable and recyclable. The logging and manufacturing processes conform to the environmental regulations of the country of origin.

Produced for A&C Black by Calcium. www.calciumcreative.co.uk

Printed and bound in China by C&C Offset Printing Co.

All the internet addresses given in this book were correct at the time of going to press. The author and publishers regret any inconvenience caused if addresses have changed or sites have ceased to exist, but can accept no responsibility for any such changes.

Acknowledgements

The publishers would like to thank the following for their kind permission to reproduce their photographs:

Cover: Fotolia: Sam Shapiro; Shutterstock: Fatih Kocyildir (front), Wikimedia Commons: Linda Spashett (back). **Pages:** Corbis: Dave Bartruff 14; Fotolia: Sam Shapiro 6, 19; Getty Images: Robert Harding World Imagery 20, Stone/Art Wolfe 11; Istockphoto: Rescigno Floriano 24; Photographers Direct: Robin Weaver 16; Rex Features: 12; Shutterstock: Galyna Andrushko 10-11, Carlos Arguelles 18-19, Vaju Ariel 5, Bond Girl 1, Amanda Haddox 3, 12-13, Xie HangXing 20-21, Mirek Hejnicki 8-9 (background), Fatih Kocyildir 6-7, 8-9, Evgeny Kovalev SPB 16-17, Giancarlo Liguori 4-5, Juriah Mosin 22-23, Tito Wong 14-15; Wikimedia Commons: E. Michael Smith 18, Linda Spashett 7, Ranveig Thattai 2-3.

Contents

Mummies! 4
Perfect Mummy 6
Mummy Home 8
Shrink It! 10
Mummy Man! 12
Still Alive 14
Bog Mummies 16
Animals, Too.......................... 18
Dead Rich 20
Glossary 22
Further Reading 23
Index 24

Mummies!

When people die, their bodies usually rot away. A mummy is a dead body that does not rot.

Mummy makers

A long time ago, people learned how to keep a body fresh by turning it into a mummy.

Dead famous

Tutankhamun is the most famous mummy ever.

Another world

People made mummies because they believed the dead went to another world and would need their bodies there.

Perfect Mummy

The Egyptians made the most famous mummies ever! They spent 70 days making each one.

What a job!
First, the mummy makers took out the body's insides. They covered the body in salt to stop it rotting. Then they **stuffed** the body.

Mummies were wrapped in strips of cloth.

Looking good

An Egyptian mummy was put in a **coffin** with a beautiful, painted mask over its face.

How do I look?

Mummy Home

The Egyptians built wonderful tombs **for important mummies, such as kings and queens.**

Amazing pyramids

Some mummy tombs are huge buildings shaped like a triangle. These are called pyramids.

Valley of Kings

Some tombs were cut into the rock. Many Egyptian kings were buried in rock tombs in a place called the Valley of the Kings in Egypt.

Mummy valley

Pharaoh Khufu's pyramid, centre, is the tallest of all.

Shrink It!

Could you wear a head as a necklace? The Jivaro people did!

Battle trophies

The Jivaro took their enemies' heads in battle. They **shrunk** the heads and sewed them shut to keep the enemies' spirits from doing harm.

Head necklace

Shrinking heads

To shrink heads, the Jivaro took out the skulls. They put the heads in hot water, then dried them with hot air.

Today the Jivaro people wear bead necklaces!

Mummy Man!

Who would want to be a mummy? Jeremy Bentham did! He lived in England about 200 years ago.

Make me a mummy

Jeremy Bentham was a **scientist** who was fascinated by mummies – he even asked to be turned into one when he died!

Jeremy's mummy can still be seen on show today.

Head case

Jeremy's head was put on show with his body. But when students stole the head and played tricks with it, a wax one was made instead!

Mummy mad!

Still Alive

Some Buddhist priests **in Japan** turned themselves into mummies!

Living mummies
The priests ate tree **bark** and drank tree **sap** tea. They knew the **poisons** in the bark and tea would kill them, but would also stop their bodies rotting when they died.

This Buddhist priest mummy can be seen in Thailand.

A happy life

Drinking and eating tree bark and sap must have been disgusting and painful! But the priests believed it would help them to be happy after they died.

Tea, anyone?

Bog Mummies

Some people became mummies when they fell into a bog!

Body story

Some bog bodies were put there on purpose. People were sometimes killed and then thrown into a bog. The body then turned into a mummy.

This mummy was found in a bog.

16

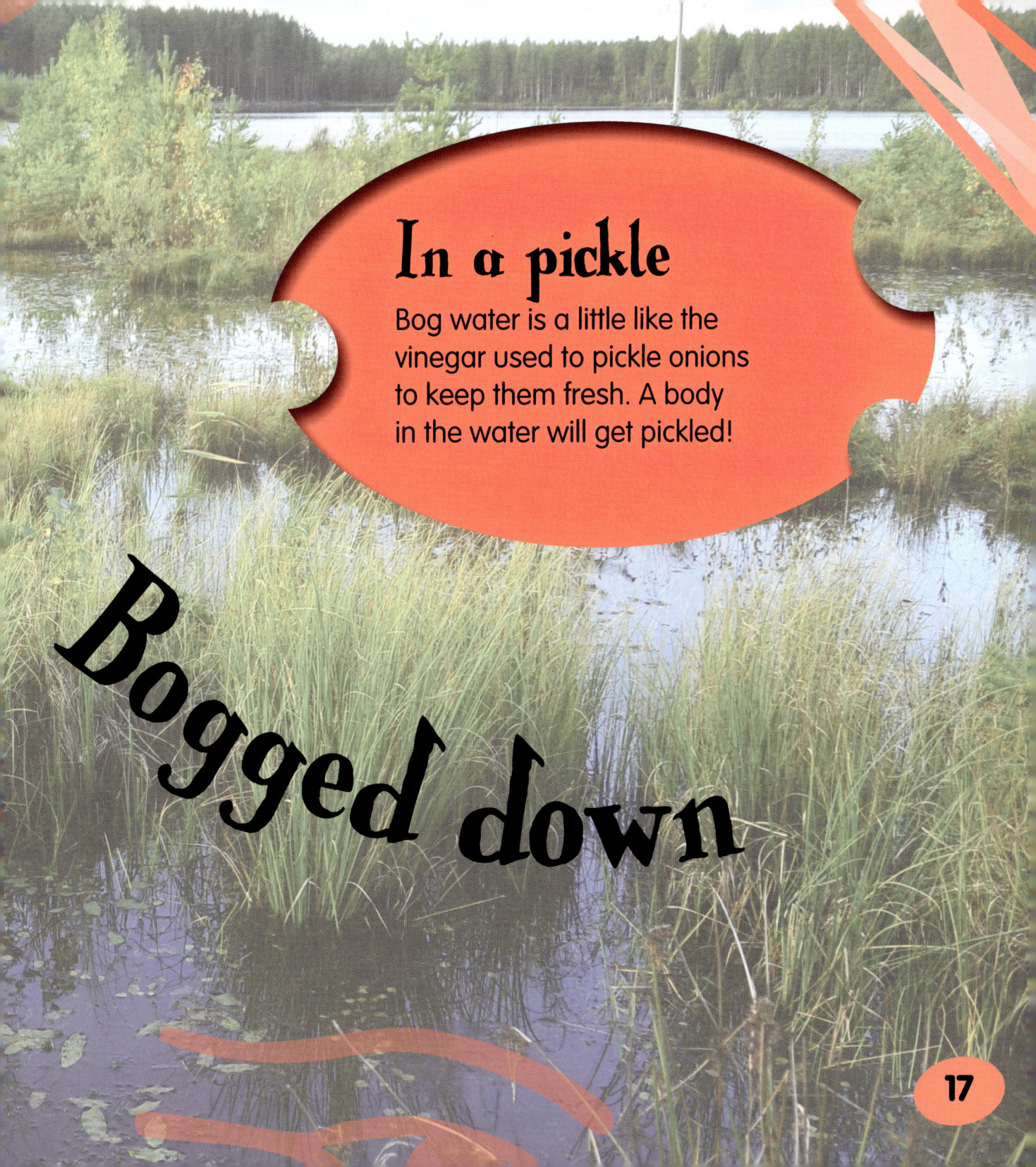

In a pickle

Bog water is a little like the vinegar used to pickle onions to keep them fresh. A body in the water will get pickled!

Bogged down

17

Animals, Too

Did you know that there are even animal mummies, too?

Pet mummies

The Egyptians thought cats were special. They even turned them into mummies and buried them with their dead owners!

The Egyptians turned dogs into mummies, too.

Mummy zoo

The Egyptians also turned birds, crocodiles, monkeys, cows, and even hippos into mummies.

Perfect pet

Dead Rich

The Egyptians buried things with their mummies.

Still need it

The Egyptians believed their mummies would need food, tools, and clothes in the next world. They buried them with the mummy.

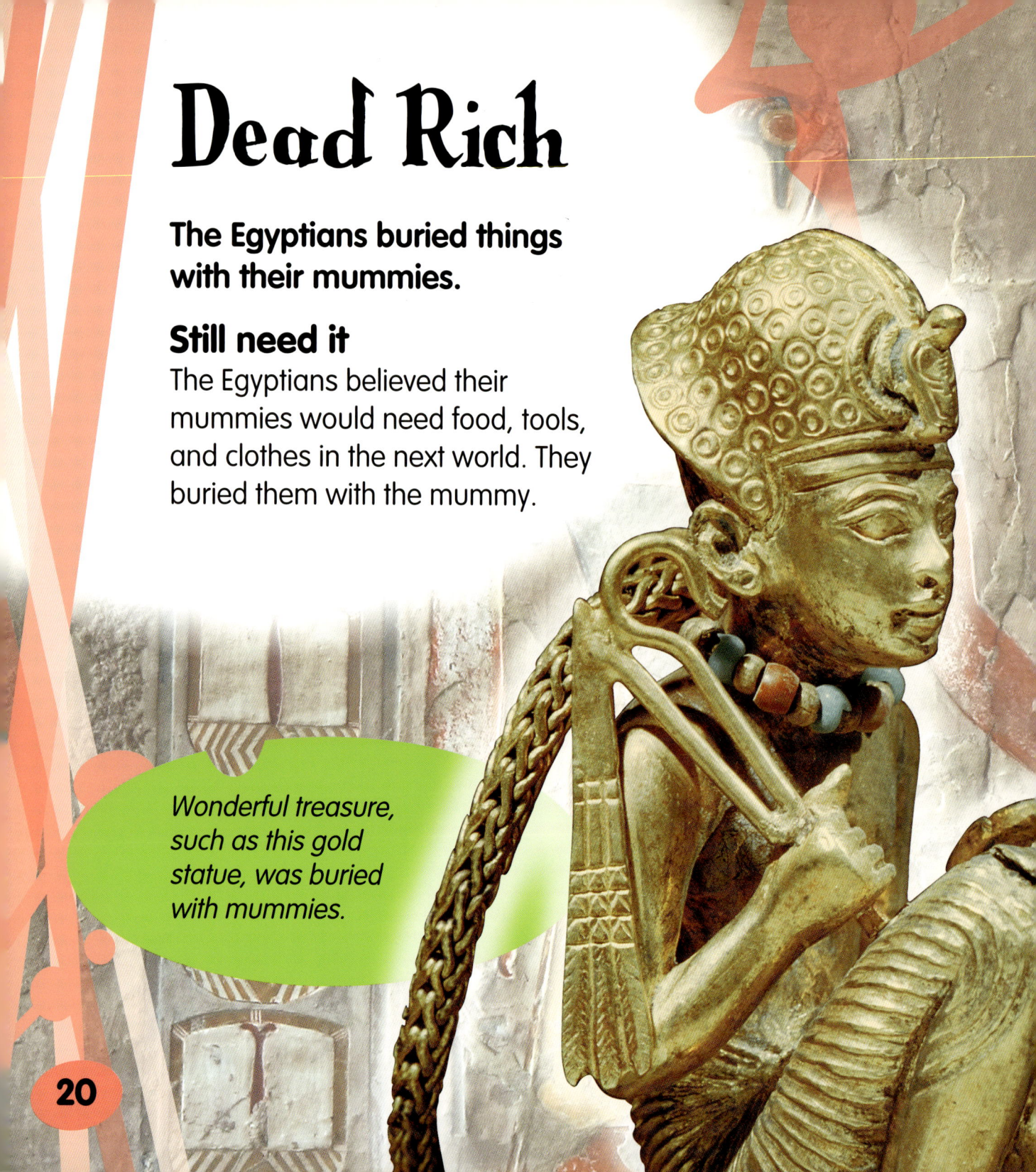

Wonderful treasure, such as this gold statue, was buried with mummies.

Not lonely

Servant statues were buried with the mummies of important people. The Egyptians believed the dead would need servants in the next life.

Treasure chest

Glossary

bark rough covering on a tree

bog a place full of watery soil

Buddhist priests people who believe in and serve a god called Buddha

coffin a special box in which a body is buried

poisons things that can make you very ill

rot to go off

sap sticky juice inside a tree

scientist a person who studies things to find out how they work

shrunk made smaller

stuffed to fill a dead body with material that keeps the body stiff

tombs buildings in which bodies are buried

Further Reading

Websites

Make your own mummy at:
kids.discovery.com/fansites/tutenstein/mummymaker.html

Find out about Egyptian mummies at:
www.ancientegypt.co.uk/mummies/index/html

Learn about mummies from all over the world at:
www.mummytombs/com/main.locator.htm

Books

Mummy (Eyewitness) by James Putnam, Dorling Kindersley (2003).

Mummies and Pyramids by Sam Taplin, Usborne Publishing (2008).

The Science of Mummy-Making by N.B. Grace, Children's Press (2009).

Index

animals 18–19

bark 14, 15
bogs 16–17
Buddhists 14–15
buried objects 20
buried people 20

cats 18
cloth 6
coffin 7

heads 10–11, 13

Jivaro 10–11

mask 7
mummies, animal 18–19
mummies, bog 16–17
mummies, living 14–15

necklaces 11

pickle 17
poisons 14
priests 14–15
pyramids 8

rot 4, 14

salt 6
sap 14, 15
scientist 12
shrunk 10
stuffed 6

tombs 8–9
treasure 20–21
Tutankhamun 5

Valley of the Kings 9